AF323578

HEAVY
Hitters

Lillenas Drama
HEAVY Hitters
11 QUICK-HIT SKETCHES FOR STAGE, STREET, AND SANCTUARY
BY LARRY AND ANNIE ENSCOE

Lillenas PUBLISHING COMPANY
KANSAS CITY, MO 64141

DEDICATION

To Mom and Dad

for whom
evanglism is a verb
(not just an idea).

You always walk what you talk.

With love
and gratitude.

Contents

Preface

Paul, we finally did it.

It has been Paul Miller's request for several years now that Team Enscoe write a book of street theatre—and we wanted to do it, sir, we really did. Well, now we finally behaved, knuckled down, and put the stuff we've been performing into some kind of recognizable sketch form.

Heavy Hitters is designed to be straightforward, quick-hit theatre. They can all be done anywhere. They're short, highly mobile, and very visual.

And the material in *Heavy Hitters* covers the full spectrum of topics—from self-esteem messages, to material designed for a churched audience, to plays meant directly for evangelism. Some are themes that play well in other countries. Some are actually adapted from stories around the world. And there are two seasonally related sketches as well.

Please let us know how they work. We'd love to hear from you.

And while you're at it, maybe drop a line to Paul Miller and tell him how much you've appreciated his ministry. None of these books you've come to enjoy over the years would be available without Paul's careful guidance, unbridled enthusiasm, and dedicated hours of labor.

God bless your time, talent, and hard work.

Larry & Annie Enscoe
Pasadena, California

Sticky Wickets

An Evangelism Sketch Without Words

Cast

ACTOR ONE: *any age, any gender*
ACTOR TWO: *any age, any gender*
ACTOR THREE: *any age, any gender*
ACTOR FOUR: *any age, any gender*
ACTOR FIVE: *any age, any gender*
ACTOR SIX: *any age, any gender*
ACTOR SEVEN: *any age, any gender*
ACTOR EIGHT: *any age, any gender*

Scene

A city street, the present

Costumes

Modern

Props

A bucket
A bucket with a Red Cross
Water
Confetti
Newspaper

Running Time

6-7 minutes

Notes

A wordless sketch on freedom from the human condition of original sin.

Production Notes

Sound effects may be used if desired.

After an audience has gathered . . .

Actor One walks into the playing area trying to get something off his hand. Something sticky. He tries to wipe it off on his other hand. On his shoe. On anything around him. It won't come off. In fact, he gets stuck to everything he touches. Have fun trying to pull your hand free of your clothes, your hair, a lamppost, or an audience member.

Actor Two comes in. He sees Actor One and waves. They walk toward each other, old friends. Actor One shakes Actor Two's hand.

Actor Two pulls his hand away. Now he's got something stuck on it. He can't get it off. He looks at Actor One—what did you just give me? Actor One shrugs innocently.

Actor Two glares, walks away. They're on opposite sides of the playing area, trying to wipe this stickiness off.

Actor Three comes onstage. He passes Actor One, who is busy wiping his hand on everything. Actor Three gives him an odd look, then sees Actor Two on the other side of the playing area. Actor Three calls out and waves.

Actor Two looks up, sees Actor Three and gives him a tentative wave. Actor Three comes over to him. Slaps him on the back. He holds out his hand to shake. Actor Two looks at Actor Three's hand, then looks at his own hand.

Actor Three grabs Actor Two's hand and vigorously shakes it. Actor Three tries to pull his hand away. He can't. Their hands are stuck together. They pull, pull, and finally fly apart.

Actor Three looks at his hand, feels the sticky on it. Looks at Actor Two with a glare.

Actor Two shrugs and points at Actor One, who is still trying to scrape sticky off his hand. Actor One looks up at them innocently—what did I do?

They both walk over to Actor One and start giving him the business. Actor One shrugs, he's sorry, doesn't know what to do.

It starts to get heated. They get "umpire" in each other's face.

Actor Two shoves Actor One at the same time Actor One shoves Actor Three at the same time Actor Three shoves Actor Two.

They're all stuck together. Like some strange square dance, they try to move, but they're all interconnected now. They run in opposite directions. They try every which way but loose.

They're stuck with each other.

Actor Four comes in. He's a do-gooder. He sees them all stuck together and decides to rescue them. He rushes toward them to help pull them apart— the three of them move away. Actor Four keeps trying to get close, but the others keep shuffling away like a six-legged creature.

Finally Actor Four shrugs and turns away, ready to leave. But then he spins around and grabs Actors Two and Three to pull them apart.

Actor Four *is now stuck.* They're now a strange eight-legged creature. All pulling opposite directions, but stuck together.

Actor Five comes in, reading a paper. He doesn't notice them. They call out to him. He looks up. Sees the eight-legged creature, throws the paper in the air, and runs out.

The eight-legged creature looks at each other.

They're all alone.

Then Actor Five comes running in with a bucket of water. He skirts the audience, barely missing them with the contents of the bucket.

He runs at the eight-legged creature, bucket ready to throw the water on them. They don't want to get wet. They keep moving away from him.

Finally, Actor Five makes one big bucket toss—but the eight-legged creature moves just in time.

Actor Five sails the contents of the bucket onto the audience.

It's confetti.

Actor Five looks at the others, who give him a "give me a break, not that old bit" look.

Actor Five shrugs at the audience and runs out.

Actor Five runs in with another bucket. He skirts the audience, almost dumping the contents on them again. He runs at the eight-legged creature. They look at each other, bored. Not this routine again. They don't move.

Actor Five *douses them with a bucket of water.*

They turn and glare at him. He throws open his hands to say—you're free. He motions for them to pull apart.

They try. They're still stuck. Actor Five frowns and comes toward them. He slips on the water and falls forward. His hands land on two of their backs. Now he's stuck with them.

It's a ten-legged creature.

They pull, tug, circle, pull, tug, circle.

Then one-by-one they lift their faces to heaven. Soon, the whole ten-legged creature is looking up to heaven.

Actor Six walks in. Sees them all looking up to heaven. He looks up to heaven with them.

Then the ten-legged creature notices Actor Six. He's still looking up to heaven. When he looks down and sees them, he jumps, startled.

They all look at each other.

Actor Six signals for them to wait here. He runs out and comes back in with another bucket.

The ten-legged creature looks at him. They shake their heads at his poor attempt. The ten-legged creature starts turning in a circle, faster, faster, faster.

Actor Six turns the bucket around so the audience can see something on the side: a red cross.

The ten-legged creature is going faster and faster. Like a whirligig. Centrifugal force builds. Actor Six looks for the right opportunity. He's getting dizzy. Finally, he tosses the bucket.

WATER hits them all and they fly apart, crashing to the ground in five different directions.

Actor Six comes over to Actor One. He extends his hand to help him up. Actor One shakes his head. Actor Six reaches down, takes his hand, and helps him up. Actor One winces, thinking they're stuck. Actor Six lets go.

They're not stuck.

Actor Six helps each surprised Actor up, one by one.

Actor One goes over and shakes Actor Two's hand. They're not stuck. They all shake each other's hands. They all walk out, arm around a shoulder, or arm in arm, or holding hands.

Actor Six smiles and walks off.

(A beat)

Actor Seven comes in. He's got something on his hand. He scrapes it on his shoe, a lamppost, a tree. It won't come off.

Actor Eight comes in. They wave at each other.

They head toward each other, hands outstretched to shake . . .

Blackout

Shortstops

Short Teaching Sketches for Kids

Hats Off

Cast

TELLER: *any age/gender*
NEW KID: *any age/gender*
KID 1: *any age/gender*
KID 2: *any age/gender*
KID 3: *any age/gender*

Scene

A schoolyard

Costumes

Modern kid

Props

Baseball caps
Signs: **A STRONG WIND, A STRONGER WIND, THE STRONGEST WIND**

Running Time

4 minutes

Notes

A short sketch that teaches how we're all the same.

Production Notes

This sketch can be performed with all kids, all adults, or mixed ages.

(Actors playing the KIDZ come in with baseball caps on forward. They're all obviously friends. They laugh, mess around, shove each other. The TELLER comes in and walks to the audience.)

TELLER: Once there was a town where all the kids wore their baseball caps forward. It was the only way to wear your cap, they said.

KID 1: Wearing your cap anyways else is totally stupid!

KIDZ: Yeah!

TELLER: See? Well, then a new kid came to school. This new kid wore his cap—

(An actor playing a NEW KID comes in. He's got his cap on backward.)

KIDZ: BACKWARD!

(The KIDZ laugh at the NEW KID. They point and imitate him. The NEW KID walks up to them.)

NEW KID: Hey, I'm new.

KID 2: Yeah, and you're a geek!

KID 3: Hat backward!

KID 1: Totally stupid!

(The KIDZ laugh at the NEW KID some more. The NEW KID looks down, sad. He walks away and stands by himself.)

TELLER: That's when a strong wind came.

*(TELLER holds up a sign that says: **A STRONG WIND**. He gets the audience to make wind noises. The KIDZ fight against the strong wind.)*

TELLER: And the wind was so strong, it blew one of their hats backward.

*(KID 3 swings his hat around backward on his head. The TELLER drops the **A STRONG WIND** sign. The audience stops making noises. KID 3 looks up, stunned.)*

KID 3: Hey!

KID 2: Hat backward!

KID 1: Totally stupid!

(The KIDZ boo and shove KID 3 out of their midst. He walks sadly over to the NEW KID. They look at each other, then shake hands. NEW KID and KID 3 look back at the other two KIDZ and laugh at them. KIDZ 1 and 2 do the same back.)

Kid 3 and New Kid: Hat forward!

Kidz 1 and 2: Hat backward!

Kidz: GEEKS!

Teller: Then a stronger wind came.

(Teller *holds up a sign that says:* **A STRONGER WIND.** *He gets the audience to make wind noises.)*

Teller: And it blew another hat backward.

(Kid 2 *swings his hat around backward. The* Teller *drops the sign. The audience stops making wind sounds.)*

Kid 2: Hey!

Kid 1: Totally stupid!

(Kid 1 *shoves* Kid 2 *away.* Kid 2 *looks down, sad. Then* New Kid *and* Kid 3 *call for him to come over and join them.* Kid 2 *smiles and runs over. They're all friends. They look back at* Kid 1 *and laugh at him.)*

New Kid/Kidz 2 and 3: Hat forward!

Kid 1 *(pointing back at them):* Totally stupid!

New Kid/Kidz 2 and 3: HAT FORWARD!

Kid 1: TOTALLY STUPID!

Teller: Then another wind came. The strongest, biggest wind of them all.

(Teller *holds up a sign that says:* **THE STRONGEST WIND.** *He gets the audience to make the wind sounds, really loud and strong.)*

Teller: And the wind blew *all* their hats off.

(*All four* Kidz *yank their hats off and throw them offstage.)*

Kidz: SWOOOOOOOSH!

Teller: And none of them had hats on, backward or forward. And they made an amazing discovery.

Kid 3: Hey!

Kid 2: No hats!

Kid 1: We're all totally the same!

New Kid: We're all kids!

(*A beat*)

Kid 3: Well . . . 'cept you have big ears.

Kɪᴅ 2: And *you* have a fat head!

Kɪᴅ 1: And your clothes look stupid!

Nᴇᴡ Kɪᴅ: And you're—

Tᴇʟʟᴇʀ: HEY! *(The* Kɪᴅᴢ *look at him. The* Tᴇʟʟᴇʀ *shakes his head.)* Totally stupid.

(The Kɪᴅᴢ *look at each other. Then they nod and throw their arms around each other's shoulders. They march off in a line, chanting.)*

Kɪᴅᴢ: Hey! Hey! Get outta our way! We just got back and we're gonna stay. Hey! Hey! Get outta our way . . . !

Blackout

Screened Out

Cast

Teller: *any age/gender*
Kid: *any age/gender*
Boy: *any age*
Girl: *any age*
Grown-up Kid: *adult, any gender*
Actors 1-7: *any ages/genders*
Same actors play Boy, Girl, and Actors 1-7

Scene

A town

Costumes

Modern

Props

Christmas box
GameBoy
Sign: **THE KID'S THOUGHT**

Running Time

4 minutes

Notes

A sketch about missing out on life—eternal and otherwise.

Production Notes

This sketch can be performed with all kids, all adults, or mixed ages.

(An actor playing a KID *opens a Christmas present. The* TELLER *comes in and looks at the audience.)*

TELLER: One Christmas, this Kid got a very cool present from his mom and dad.

(The KID *pulls out a GameBoy.)*

KID: Whoa! Thanks, Mom! Thanks, Dad! You guys are the best!

(The KID *jumps up and starts playing. He's completely mesmerized. He turns into a screenkid.)*

TELLER: And this Kid loved his new game. He played it wherever he went. And he went wherever he could play it. You gotta admit, it was a very cool Christmas gift.

(The KID *walks along, his face glued to the screen, his fingers working the keys. The* KID *passes a* BOY *and* GIRL *looking in a river. They look up and see the* KID.*)*

BOY: Hey, Kid! C'mover here and look in this river!

GIRL: Yeah! We're lookin' at tadpoles and stuff!

(The KID *keeps walking by, doesn't even hear them.)*

TELLER: But the Kid didn't even hear the Boy and the Girl. All he could hear was . . .

(The KID *makes computer game noises.)*

TELLER: And the Kid kept playing that game night and day. He couldn't stop.

(The KID *walks through a gauntlet of* ACTORS *playing a variety of people in his life. He doesn't look up at any of them as they speak.)*

ACTOR 1: Put that thing away and go to sleep.

ACTOR 2: Who's playing a computer game in my class?

ACTOR 3: Wanna play baseball with us?! Wanna play basketball? *(Disgusted)* Wanna play in traffic?

ACTOR 4: Can you please pass me the milk? Hey, are you listening! PLEASE PASS ME THE MILK!

ACTOR 5: Look both ways before you cross the street!

ACTOR 6: Get your face outta that thing! It'll ruin your eyes!

ACTOR 7: Your brains are gonna turn to mush!

ACTOR 8: Look out! You're gonna step in—

(The KID *steps in something. He stops.)*

ALL ACTORS: Ewwwwwwww.

(The KID looks on the bottom of his shoe and grimaces.)

TELLER: Then one morning, the Kid had a thought.

(The KID looks up, sees an ACTOR come in wearing a sign that says: **THE KID'S THOUGHT.**)

KID'S THOUGHT ACTOR: "Why am I here?"

TELLER: But the Kid had a three-headed monster he had to blow up real good. And the thought went away.

(The KID looks back at his screen and walks by, brushing the KID'S THOUGHT ACTOR aside.)

TELLER: Then, a few days later, the Kid had another thought.

(The KID stops, looks up and sees an ACTOR come in wearing a sign that says: **THE KID'S THOUGHT.**)

KID'S THOUGHT ACTOR: "Is there a God? Does God love me?"

TELLER: But the Kid was in the middle of a fight with an evil flesh-eating dwarf, and he had to kick him out of the castle in order to get to the next level. So the thought went away.

(The KID looks back at the screen and walks by, brushing the KID'S THOUGHT ACTOR aside.)

TELLER: And the Kid grew up—

(A GROWN-UP KID comes in and passes the KID, who hands off the GameBoy to him and goes offstage. GROWN-UP KID now plays the GameBoy, face glued to the screen. He wears grown-up versions of the KID's clothes.)

TELLER: And the Grownup Kid got to all kinds of next levels—except in real life. And then one day, something sad happened.

(The GROWN-UP KID steps out into the street.)

VOICES: LOOK OUT! LOOK OUT!

(The VOICES make the sound of a car squealing and then a car CRASH. The GROWN-UP KID drops the GameBoy. He falls down. Then he gets back up. He looks around.)

TELLER: The Grown-up Kid got to the next level, all right. The Final Level.

GROWN-UP KID: Hey, how do I reset? I wanna start over!

(He picks up the GameBoy and thumbs keys, then punches the keys, then hammers the keys.)

TELLER: But he couldn't reset. He couldn't reload. He couldn't reboot.

GROWN-UP KID: Wait!

(The GROWN-UP KID and the TELLER look at each other.)

TELLER: Game over, man.

Blackout

The Girl Who Wouldn't Cry

Cast

TELLER: *any age/gender*
AUSTIN: *female, any age*
BRITTANY: *female, any age*
BOY 1: *male, any age*
BOY 2: *male, any age*
KIDS 1-3: *any age/gender*
BRITTANY'S MOM: *female, 20s to 40s*
Same actors play AUSTIN, BOYS, and KIDS.

Scene

Schoolyard, town, home

Costumes

Modern

Props

A tub with sign: **TEARS**
Blue confetti

Running Time

4 minutes

Notes

This sketch is about finding a safe person to show your emotions to.

Production Notes

This sketch can be performed with all kids, all adults, or mixed ages.

TELLER: One day, two little girls were walking down the street. One was named Austin and one was named Brittany.

(Two actors come in playing little GIRLS. They're laughing and talking. They pass two actors playing two little BOYS.)

TELLER: And right in front of two boys, Austin fell down.

AUSTIN: Whoa!

(AUSTIN falls down.)

TELLER: And it hurt. So she cried.

(AUSTIN starts crying. The two BOYS look over at her.)

BOY 1: Baby!

BOY 2: Baby!

(This makes AUSTIN cry even more.)

TELLER: And when Brittany saw how Austin got treated when she cried, she decided:

BRITTANY: I'm never gonna cry again as long as I live!

TELLER: And Brittany was true to her word. She never cried. No matter what happened.

(BRITTANY walks along. A BOY trips her and she falls.)

BOY: Whoops! You fell down!

TELLER: But Brittany didn't cry.

(BRITTANY gets up, looks at the BOY, and keeps walking. ANOTHER KID shoves her.)

ANOTHER KID: Watch where you're goin'!

(BRITTANY looks at the KID and keeps walking.)

TELLER: And Brittany kept on not crying.

(A GIRL watches her go by.)

GIRL *(singsong)*: Brittany's uuu-gly and stooo-pid!

(BRITTANY keeps walking, she doesn't cry.)

TELLER: And still Brittany didn't cry. It wasn't long before Brittany couldn't cry at anything. A sad part on a TV show, when someone she loved got hurt, or when she saw how bad the latest Power Rangers movie was and she'd already used up her allowance to get in.

BRITTANY: I'm not gonna cry! I'm not gonna be a baby!

TELLER: And all those tears had nowhere to go. So they stayed inside Brittany. And she began to swell up like a big sad balloon.

(BRITTANY *pooches out her face and mimes like she's turned into a huge balloon, walking like a sumo wrestler.*)

TELLER: Of course, this made everybody even meaner to her.

KID 1: Brittany's fat!

KID 2: Brittany's huge!

KID 3: Brittany's fat and huge!

(*They all squeal like a pig. But* BRITTANY *doesn't cry. She just keeps waddling on.*)

TELLER: Everybody could hear something when Brittany walked by.

EVERYONE: Slosh, slosh, slosh!

TELLER: But they didn't know what it was.

EVERYONE: Sloshsloshslosh—HEY WHAT'S THAT NOISE? Sloshsloshslosh.

TELLER: They didn't know it was all those tears like a big huge ocean inside of Brittany.

(BRITTANY *mimes waddling into her house from school. Everyone keeps saying: "sloshsloshsloshslosh." Her* MOM *comes in and looks at her.*)

TELLER: Then, one day, her mom asked:

BRITTANY'S MOM: Brittany, honey, you look so sad. What's the matter?

BRITTANY: I'm not gonna cry!

BRITTANY'S MOM: You can cry if you want to, Brittany.

BRITTANY: Crying's for babies.

BRITTANY'S MOM: Who told you that?

BRITTANY: One day Austin fell down and everyone called her a baby!

BRITTANY'S MOM: You haven't cried since then?

(BRITTANY *shakes her head.*)

BRITTANY'S MOM: You haven't wanted to cry?

(BRITTANY *shakes her head. Then she hears in her mind.*)

KIDS: Whoops, you fell down!
      Hey, watch where yer goin'!
      Brittany's uuu-gly and stooo-pid!
      Huge and fat! Huge and fat!

(BRITTANY *starts to cry—but stops herself. Her tears are building up.*)

BRITTANY: Not gonna cry!

BRITTANY'S MOM: It's OK to cry, Brittany.

BRITTANY: Not gonna cry!

BRITTANY'S MOM: But you don't have to cry in front of anyone you don't want to.

BRITTANY: Not gonna cry!

BRITTANY'S MOM: Find someone you can cry in front of. Find someone who will understand and not make fun of you.

BRITTANY: Who?

BRITTANY'S MOM: Me.

BRITTANY: WHAAAAAAA!

BRITTANY'S MOM: I love you, sweetheart.

(BRITTANY *starts crying up a storm. Her* MOM *puts her arms around her.*)

TELLER: And Brittany cried and cried.

BRITTANY: WHAAAAAAAAA!

TELLER: All that time without crying made a lot of tears inside her.

(*Three* KIDS *come in struggling with a huge tub that says:* **TEARS**.)

BRITTANY: WHAAAAAAAA!

(*The three* KIDS *pick up the tub and dump it on* BRITTANY *and her* MOM *[it's blue confetti].*)

BRITTANY'S MOM: Brittany . . . uh, honey . . . Mommy and Daddy don't have flood insurance.

(BRITTANY *looks at her* MOM—*and starts laughing.*)

TELLER: Then Brittany realized something. All those tears inside her had drowned all the laughter too.

BRITTANY: HAHAHAHAHAHAHAHAAHA!

(BRITTANY *picks up a handful of confetti and throws it in the air.* BRITTANY'S MOM *joins in. So do the* KIDS. *They all laugh and throw confetti into the air right up to the . . .)*

Blackout

Where Does It Hurt?

An Evangelism Sketch Without Words

Cast

MAN: *any age*
DOCTOR: *any age*

Scene

A street, the present

Costumes

Comic modern

Props

Doctor's coat
Black bag
Paper that says: **SUMMONS**
Paper that says: **DOCTOR'S LICENSE**
Sign that says: **CONSCIENCE**
2 wristwatches
Reflex hammer
Flashlight
Eye chart
Ugly glasses
Stethoscope
Heart-shaped box
Paper that says: **DOCTOR'S BILL**

Running Time

5 minutes

Notes

This is an evangelistic sketch on spiritual emptiness. It's performed in a broad slapstick style.

Production Notes

Feel free to use sound effects.

After a crowd gathers . . .

A MAN comes through the crowd into the playing area. Suddenly, he clutches his chest and starts weaving. He's in great pain. Oy, it hurts.

He reels this way. He reels that way. He looks up to heaven. He collapses against onlookers, then pulls himself away. He falls to the ground. Twitches up, falls back. Twitches up, falls back. Frowns and sits up. There's a stone under him. He picks it up, throws it, scoots over a little, and lays back. He starts twitching up and falling back.

Madame Butterfly didn't die this big.

Finally, he falls back. Still. Then he sits up, looks at the way he's lying on the ground. Doesn't like it. He crosses one leg over his ankle. Adjusts his jacket. Unbuttons a shirt button. That's better.

Then he falls back. He's out.

(A beat)

A DOCTOR pushes his way through the crowd. He sees the MAN lying there. He motions for the crowd to back up a bit. Give him room to work. Back up, man, he's a scientist. He motions that he has proof he's a doctor. He pats his pockets. Finds a piece of paper. He smiles, pulls it out, and opens it up. It says **SUMMONS** on it. He quickly puts that away. Pats his pockets, finds another paper. Pulls it out and shows the crowd. It says **DOCTOR'S LICENSE.**

The DOCTOR walks over to the MAN. Starts to examine him. He pulls out one pocket. Then the other. Empty pockets. He frowns at the crowd.

Then he examines some more and finds the MAN's wallet. He eyeballs it. Turns it over. Opens it up. Nothing inside. He turns it over and shakes it. Nothing.

DOCTOR frowns. Puts the wallet back. Motions to the crowd that the MAN is obviously dead. He wipes his hands and starts to walk away.

OUCH! Something sticks the DOCTOR in his back pocket. He reaches in, pulls out a small sign. It's covered with dust. He blows off the dust—it sends off a duststorm. He reads the sign.

It says **CONSCIENCE.**

The DOCTOR starts to throw the sign. Then stops. He sighs, puts the sign in his back pocket, and walks back to the MAN lying there.

The DOCTOR pulls off the MAN's shoe. Examines the bottom of his foot.

The MAN giggles at the tickle.

DOCTOR looks up. MAN stops giggling and is perfectly still. DOCTOR goes back to the foot.

The MAN giggles at the tickle.

The DOCTOR looks up. The MAN stops. The DOCTOR is suspicious now. He tickles the MAN's foot.

The MAN sits up, laughing like mad, begs the DOCTOR to stop. The DOCTOR gives him a look and stops. He takes out his little hammer. He taps on the MAN's knee. The MAN's arm jerks and smacks the DOCTOR. He goes flying back.

The DOCTOR gets up. Walks over to the MAN. Wants to know what's wrong with him. The MAN shrugs, he doesn't know.

The DOCTOR grabs the MAN's wrist to take his pulse. He doesn't see he's put his fingers on the MAN's watchband. The DOCTOR checks the pulse against his own watch.

The DOCTOR looks alarmed. The MAN has no pulse!

The DOCTOR shrugs and pushes the guy back down on the ground and closes his eyes.

The MAN sits up—hey, I'm alive!

The DOCTOR shakes his head, points at the MAN's wrist, and signals no pulse. You're a flatliner. He pushes the MAN back down on the ground.

The MAN pops up and points to his wrist. He's got a wristwatch on. The DOCTOR looks twice, then his shoulders shrug with laughter. He takes off the MAN's watch.

The DOCTOR grabs the MAN's watch-less wrist and starts to take his pulse. The DOCTOR looks at his watch. Looks at the MAN. He can't believe it—no pulse again!

Then the DOCTOR looks at his watch and shrugs with laughter again. The DOCTOR takes off his own watch and shakes it. Pounds it. It's stopped.

The DOCTOR puts the MAN's watch on his own wrist and puts the broken one back on the MAN's wrist.

The MAN starts to protest.

The DOCTOR grabs the MAN's head and checks for bumps. Then he shines a flashlight in each eye. When he pulls the flashlight away—the MAN's blind. Can't see anything.

The DOCTOR takes out an eye chart and holds it up and away for the MAN to read. The MAN can't see anything, he's blinded by the light. The DOCTOR keeps holding the chart closer and closer. The MAN can't see.

The DOCTOR shrugs, opens his black bag, and takes out an ugly pair of glasses and puts them on the MAN.

Then the DOCTOR opens his bag and pulls out all kinds of strange and scary instruments, including a hand mixer. Finally, he finds a stethoscope.

He checks the MAN's heartbeat.

The DOCTOR looks surprised.

Then curious.

Then amazed.

The DOCTOR pulls out a huge pair of scissors. The MAN freaks. The DOCTOR calms him down, then reaches the scissors under the MAN's coat—snip, snip, snip. He cuts off the buttons of his shirt. Then reaches inside the MAN's shirt

. . .

The DOCTOR pulls out the MAN's Heart (it's a heart-shaped cardboard box). The DOCTOR holds it in a way that makes it look like it's really beating.

The DOCTOR opens up the heart—it's empty. Nothing inside. The DOCTOR points inside the heart—there's your problem. He hands the MAN back his heart.

The MAN looks inside his own heart. He can't believe it. He runs his finger around inside. He pulls his finger out. He looks at his finger. Then blows off the dust.

The MAN shouts "HELLO!" into his heart. There's an echo—"HELLO! . . . Hello . . . hello . . ."

The MAN shouts "ANYONE HOME!" into his heart. There's an echo—"ANYONE! . . . Anyone . . . anyone . . ."

The MAN starts crying. He looks at the DOCTOR—what can I do?

The DOCTOR shrugs, palms up—not my department.

The DOCTOR pulls out a piece of paper that says **DOCTOR'S BILL.** He writes on it, then hands it to the MAN.

The MAN looks at the total.

The MAN's heart jumps out of his hands.

The DOCTOR picks up his black bag and starts to walk away. He stops. He forgot something. He remembers and snaps his fingers.

He walks back to the MAN, grabs his heart, stuffs it back inside his shirt, and buttons up his jacket.

The DOCTOR wipes his hands and walks away.

The MAN calls after him! The DOCTOR keeps walking. The MAN calls after him!

The DOCTOR is gone.

The MAN sits there, miserable. He hears KNOCKING. He looks around. The sound of KNOCKING. He looks at his heart. More KNOCKING.

The MAN reaches into his shirt and takes out his own heart.

He listens to the heart. More KNOCKING. It's not coming from his heart.

He looks around. More KNOCKING. He listens to the ground. More KNOCKING. He looks up. More KNOCKING. He nods.

The KNOCKING comes from above him.

The MAN lifts his heart up toward heaven.

And he opens it.

Blackout

Acts like a Dog, Thinks like a Dog, Must Be a Dog

A Sketch on Self-esteem

Cast

HUSBAND: *20s to 50s*
WIFE: *20s to 50s*
MAX: *12-year-old boy or adult playing younger*
GUEST: *any age*

Scene

A dining room, the present

Costumes

Modern

Props

Table
Four chairs
Cutlery
Dishware

Running Time

6-7 minutes

Notes

This short sketch explores the idea of how people may choose to see us—and how God knows us.

(A table and three chairs. HUSBAND *enters, carrying dishware and cutlery. He's setting the table.)*

HUSBAND: Time's our guest coming for dinner?

WIFE *(off):* Seven o'clock.

*(*WIFE *enters carrying plates of food. She sets the food on the table.)*

WIFE: This is the first time he's been over, you know.

HUSBAND: I know.

WIFE *(calling off):* Max!

HUSBAND: Been meaning to ask him over for a long time.

WIFE: I know. *(Calling off)* MAX!

(A 12-year-old boy bounds in on all fours. This is MAX. *He sniffs around. Sniffs their feet.)*

HUSBAND: Good Max. Good boy.

*(*MAX *wags his "tail." He jumps up on the chair.)*

WIFE: No, Max! Get off the furniture!

HUSBAND: Down, Max!

*(*MAX *looks hurt and jumps off the chair.* WIFE *goes out of the room.* HUSBAND *makes sure she's gone, then leans down to* MAX.*)*

HUSBAND: 'bout a treat, huh, Max?

*(*MAX *brightens, wags his "tail."* HUSBAND *grabs a "treat" off the table, holds it over* MAX*'s head.)*

HUSBAND: Talk!

*(*MAX *prances in a circle.)*

HUSBAND: *Talk!*

*(*MAX *barks once.* HUSBAND *gives* MAX *the treat.* MAX *hungrily eats it down.* WIFE *comes in.)*

WIFE: You're not supposed to feed him off the table!

HUSBAND *(startled):* I know, but he—

WIFE: He'll get fat. He'll get bad habits. Bad Max!

*(*MAX *droops his head. There's a knock, off.)*

WIFE: He's here!

HUSBAND: Our guest!

(HUSBAND *and* WIFE *go offstage.* MAX *looks, sniffs around. Then he climbs up in the chair and sniffs the food. He starts to eat something off a plate. He's obviously hungry.* HUSBAND *and* WIFE *come in with the* GUEST.)

GUEST: You really have a beautiful home here.

WIFE *(glowing):* Well, thank you.

HUSBAND: Been meaning to ask you over for a long—

WIFE *(sees* MAX*):* MAX!

(MAX *leaps down off the chair, mortified. Head low, waiting for punishment.*)

HUSBAND: Bad boy!

WIFE: Go to your corner!

HUSBAND: Corner, now!

(MAX *drags over to the corner, head slung low.*)

WIFE: *Sit.*

HUSBAND: Sit, bad boy!

(MAX *sits, head still low.* WIFE *turns to the* GUEST, *who looks stunned.*)

WIFE: I'm so sorry.

HUSBAND: Very embarrassing.

WIFE: We're trying to train him to be a good boy.

HUSBAND: Usually a good boy.

WIFE: He has his own food . . . *(Loud so* MAX *can hear)* . . . he's not supposed to touch *ours.*

HUSBAND: Bad habits!

(HUSBAND *holds out the chair to the* GUEST, *who sits, still uncomfortable with what's going on.*)

HUSBAND: Please, sit right here.

WIFE: I'll go get the salads

HUSBAND: I'll help.

WIFE *(glaring at* MAX*):* Stay there.

HUSBAND: *Stay.*

(HUSBAND *and* WIFE *leave.* GUEST *turns to* MAX.)

GUEST: Max? Max? (MAX *doesn't look up.*) Max, do your parents know you're not a dog?

(MAX *looks up. Their eyes meet.*)

GUEST: Do they know you're a boy?

(MAX *barks.* HUSBAND *and* WIFE *sweep in with salads.*)

WIFE: You and Max getting to know each other?

GUEST: Yes, uh, we—

HUSBAND: Let's eat!

(*They sit down and pick up their forks. The* GUEST *doesn't pick up his.*)

WIFE: What's the matter?

HUSBAND: Fork dirty?

GUEST: No, it's just . . . well, where's Max's chair?

WIFE: Max doesn't have a chair!

HUSBAND: Max's got a bed. Back room.

GUEST: No, I mean a chair. At the table.

WIFE: Oh, no. Max isn't allowed on the furniture.

HUSBAND: Can't eat off the table.

GUEST: Why? He's your son.

(HUSBAND *and* WIFE *look at each other.*)

WIFE: Does he act like a dog?

GUEST: Yes.

HUSBAND: Talk like a dog?

GUEST: Yes.

WIFE: Think like a dog?

GUEST: Well, yes, because you—

WIFE: Then he's a dog.

HUSBAND: Max, talk! *Talk!*

(MAX *barks.*)

HUSBAND: Good boy!

GUEST (*gets up*): I'd like Max to sit in my chair.

WIFE: Max can't get on the furniture!

GUEST: Then I'm afraid I'll have to go.

HUSBAND: You're our guest!

WIFE: We made dinner!

GUEST: I'm sorry.

WIFE: But Max is very happy being a dog!

HUSBAND: Always has been.

GUEST: I'm afraid I have to insist.

(*It's a standoff. Finally the* WIFE *looks at* MAX.)

WIFE: Max, get on the chair.

(MAX *looks at her, can't believe it.*)

HUSBAND: Good boy, on the chair!

(MAX *bounds up on the chair.* GUEST *helps* MAX *sit like a human, straightens his legs, pulls the chair up to the table, puts a fork in his hand.* MAX *is amazed. He's sitting like a real boy.*)

WIFE: He won't be happy sitting like that.

HUSBAND: We'd know.

WIFE: We're his parents.

GUEST: Max needs some food.

WIFE: Max has food.

HUSBAND: In his bowl.

GUEST: Max needs a salad. Should I give him mine?

WIFE: No!

HUSBAND: Made it for *you!*

(*Another standoff*)

WIFE: All right, I'll go get Max a salad.

HUSBAND: I'll help!

(HUSBAND *and* WIFE *leave, whispering to each other.*)

GUEST: You're not a dog, are you? Talk.

MAX: I . . . m not a d . . . og.

GUEST: Don't let anyone tell you different, Max. God made you a boy. Strong, smart, a good heart. That's who you are, Max. You're a boy.

MAX: I'm a boy.

GUEST: That's right. *(Holds out his hand)* Shake.

*(*MAX *holds out his paw.* GUEST *takes* MAX's *hand, opens the fingers, and helps him clasp his hand around his own. They shake.* GUEST *smiles at* MAX. *Then* GUEST *leaves.* HUSBAND *and* WIFE *come in with a salad bowl and another chair. They look around.)*

WIFE: Where'd our guest go?

HUSBAND: He left?

WIFE *(looks at* MAX*)*: Did you scare him off?

*(*MAX *shakes his head.)*

WIFE: Get down off the furniture.

HUSBAND: Down, boy!

*(*MAX *looks at them.)*

MAX: I'm not a dog.

*(*HUSBAND *and* WIFE *look at each other. Their mouths drop open.)*

Blackout

Keeping Mum

An Evangelism Sketch Without Words

Cast

HOBO ONE: *any age/gender*
HOBO TWO: *any age/gender*
ACTOR 1: *any age/gender*
ACTOR 2: *any age/gender*

Scene

A deserted place, the present

Costumes

Hobo costumes, realistic or abstracted

Props

Large rock
Small rock
Dried bush
Faded red scarf
Styrofoam burger container
Sign that says: **AGE** on one side and **A.M.** on the other
Sign that says: **MIR** on one side and **P.M.** on the other
Bread

Running Time

6-7 minutes

Notes

This sketch is a hard-hitting look at the power of the Bread of Life to restore—
and the devastation when it is not shared.

Production Notes

Even though this is a dark sketch, the performance tone is slapstick comic, until the last few moments. The bread used in our performance was made out of angel food cake. It makes it easier to eat fast with an audience staring at you.

Lights.

The playing area has a large rock, a small rock, and a dried bush. A faded red scarf wrapped around something, out of sight of the actors, but visible to the audience.

A train's WHISTLE, long and mournful. Then the sound of a TRAIN PASSING, loud.

HOBO ONE jumps into the playing area and rolls, as if he jumped from the train.

HOBO TWO jumps into the playing area and rolls. He crashes onto HOBO ONE. HOBO ONE shoves him off. HOBO TWO looks at him, shrugs an apology.

The TRAIN sound FADES. Gone.

HOBO ONE and HOBO TWO stand. They pat themselves down, looking for broken bones. No damage. They sigh and look around. Nothing for miles.

They look at each other. HOBO ONE points off, suggesting a direction they take. HOBO TWO nods. They start walking, exhausted.

The sound of something GROWLING.

They both jump. They circle, back-to-back, looking for the wild animal.

GROWLING again.

They stop. Straighten. Look at each other.

GROWLING again.

HOBO ONE points to HOBO TWO's stomach. HOBO TWO points to HOBO ONE's stomach.

GROWLING again.

They both look at their own stomachs.

GROWLING again.

They both jump at the sound of their own hunger. They look at each other, mournfully. They pat themselves down, nothing. They pull their pockets inside-out, empty.

GROWLING again. Loud. They both grab their stomachs and drop to the ground. They sit there. Too hungry to move.

GROWLING again.

They lay back on the ground.

TWO ACTORS come in with signs. They say **A.M.** and **P.M.** They pass across the back of the playing area several times to show passing time. Then the ACTORS come together with their signs, so they say **A.M./P.M.**

HOBO ONE and HOBO TWO sit up. They see the sign like a beacon in the wilderness. **A.M./P.M.** MiniMart! They sit up. Reach for the sign. Start crawling toward it.

Then the ACTORS turn their signs around. One signs says **AGE**. The other says **MIR**. Put together they spell **AGEMIR**. The ACTORS look at the signs. They glare at each other and change positions. Now they spell **MIRAGE**.

The Actors laugh and run off.

Hobo One and Hobo Two look at each other. They rub their eyes and look back to where the sign was.

Nothing's there.

They look at each other. GROWLING again. They both fall back.

Then they see something at the same time: a Styrofoam fast-food hamburger container, just sitting there.

They look at each other. Neither one moves. They eagle-eye each other, trying to see who will move first.

Suddenly, they both spring at once, scrabbling toward the container. They grab it at the same time, tearing it in half. One has the top, one has the bottom.

It's empty. Nothing inside. Not so much as a catsup stain.

They look at each other, stunned. They both lick the inside of the container half they're holding. They drop them on the ground. Then they eye the half the other has dropped. At the same time they grab the other's half and lick the inside of those too.

Then they look at the container halves. They look at each other. They both bite into the spongy material. They chew it a minute, then make a face and spit it out.

They drop the container halves.

The TRAIN WHISTLE again. They both look up at the train coming. Then the sound of the TRAIN PASSING. They both try to crawl toward it. Both too weak. Can't make it more then a few feet.

The sound of the TRAIN PASSING and FADING. Gone.

Hobo One shakes his head. It's no use. He drops his head to the ground. Lies there. He's so still. Hobo Two looks at Hobo One. Hobo One doesn't move for a long time.

Hobo Two waves to get his attention.

Hobo One doesn't look up.

Hobo Two "calls" him.

Hobo One doesn't look up.

Hobo Two crawls over to him. Stares at him. Then reaches out his hand, slowly. Shakes him.

Hobo One doesn't look up.

Hobo Two freaks out. Thinks he's dead. He grabs Hobo One and shakes him.

Hobo One wakes up and throws him off. They stare at each other. Hobo One waves him off, wants to be left alone.

Hobo Two crawls away, hurt. His stomach GROWLS again. He looks down at it. Then he looks up to heaven. He gets on his knees, folds his hands, and prays. Fervently. He begs, pleads, wails.

Then he sees it.

A faded red scarf.

Hobo Two looks up to heaven, questioning. Then he crawls over and pokes the red scarf. He picks it up. Smells it. Unties it. Opens it up.

A piece of bread falls out.

Hobo Two stares at it, stunned. He picks it up. He can't believe what he sees. He licks it. It *is* bread.

He grins. He laughs. He holds the chunk of bread up to heaven in jubilant thanksgiving.

Then Hobo Two digs in. He starts wolfing the bread down. Another bite, another bite, another bite—

Hobo One groans in his sleep.

Hobo Two stops in mid-chew. He looks over and sees Hobo One stir. Hobo Two looks at the bread in his hand. He feels a pang of conscience and divides the piece of bread in half. He sets one half down on the red scarf for Hobo One, then ravenously eats his half, licking his fingers and palms to catch every crumb.

Hobo Two stands. His energy has come back with the food. He feels great. Never felt so good.

Then Hobo Two sees the other half of the bread. He looks at Hobo One, still asleep. He looks back at the bread. Back at Hobo One. Hobo Two hesitantly reaches for the bread. Hobo One stirs.

Hobo Two jumps up, backs away from the bread.

But Hobo One doesn't awaken.

Hobo Two creeps toward the bread, eyeing Hobo One the whole way. Suddenly, Hobo Two pounces on the bread, snatching it up and eating it down. He sits back on his haunches to finish the last little bit, smacking his lips as he does so.

Hobo One stirs noiselessly. He awakens. He sees Hobo Two sitting there, smacking his lips.

Hobo Two turns and sees Hobo One staring at him. He jumps, startled, caught. They stare at each other. Menace in the air.

Suddenly Hobo One is on his feet. He comes for Hobo Two—who grabs the red scarf, stuffs it in his coat pocket, and gets up to run.

Hobo One whistles. Hobo Two freezes in his tracks. Hobo One beckons Hobo Two over.

Hobo Two sidles up to Hobo One, nervously. Hobo One motions for Hobo Two to open his mouth.

Hobo Two shakes his head "no."

Hobo One urgently motions for Hobo Two to open his mouth.

Hobo Two shakes his head "no."

Hobo One grabs Hobo Two and tugs on his mouth. Hobo Two struggles against him. Finally, Hobo One pries Hobo Two's mouth open.

Hobo One sniffs Hobo Two's breath. He peers down his throat with one eye. Then he sticks a finger in his mouth and wipes around. He pulls his finger back and smells it. He licks it.

Bread.

Hobo One knocks Hobo Two to the ground. Hobo Two tries to crawl away. Hobo One is all over him, sticking his hands in his pockets, searching for bread. Hobo One finds the red scarf. He pulls it out. Looks at it. Shakes it out into his hand. No crumbs. He puts the scarf to his face and inhales the smell of bread, now long gone.

Hobo One leans against a rock, utter despair. Then he starts to weep noiselessly.

Hobo Two doesn't know what to do. He tries to beg forgiveness. Hobo One doesn't even see him. He just curls up and closes his eyes. He doesn't move.

Hobo Two stands there, staring at Hobo One. He looks around. Nudges Hobo One with his foot.

Hobo One doesn't stir.

Hobo Two nudges him again.

Hobo One doesn't move.

Then the sound of the TRAIN WHISTLE.

Hobo Two looks up. Sees the train coming. He looks down at Hobo One once more.

Then Hobo Two runs offstage after the train.

Hobo One just lays there, unmoving.

The sound of the TRAIN PASSES and FADES. Gone.

Hobo One doesn't move. Silence.

Blackout

Kingdom Haul

A Sketch on Not Taking It with You

Cast

Bwana: *any age/gender*
Lump: *any age/gender*

Scene

Outside the Kingdom

Costumes

Modern

Props

A tunnel (wall with a hole cut in it)
Signs that say: **THE KINGDOM, KINGDOM HERE! THIS IS IT! YOU FOUND IT! KINGDOM THIS WAY!**
Red wagon
Stuff: TV, blender, golf clubs
Duffel bags
Train case
Suitcases
Binoculars
Pith helmet
Camera
Kazoo

Running Time

8 minutes

Notes

A funny twist on not taking it with you.

Production Notes

The tunnel needs to be strong enough for an actor to crawl through and tall enough for him not to be seen on the other side of it.

(Lights. Onstage sits a tunnel, or a wall with a hole cut into it. The entrance/hole should be at the actor's waist level. Signs around the stage say: **KINGDOM HERE! THIS IS IT! YOU FOUND IT! KINGDOM THIS WAY!**

(LUMP *enters pulling a red wagon. Baggy pants, several coats, wig and hat. He looks like Harpo Marx. He lugs several duffel bags, beat-up suitcases, backpacks, and a bag of golf clubs. He should look like a beast of burden. The wagon is crammed with the stuff of life: TVs, appliances, CDs, a Christmas tree stand, etc.*

(LUMP *wanders like he's in a jungle. Then he sees a sign.* **THE KINGDOM.** *He points at it, dances a jig. Then he sees the tunnel. He goes to it and looks inside. He looks at us, grave doom on his face.)*

VOICE *(off):* LUMP!

(LUMP *hears the voice and jumps. He pulls the wagon behind a sign and hides.* BWANA *stomps in, staring through a pair of binoculars. Wearing jodhpurs, boots, a dusty old tuxedo coat, a pith helmet. He has a duffel bag over his shoulder and a train case in hand. An instamatic camera hangs around his neck.)*

BWANA: Lump? Where are you? Are you hiding from me, Lumpy? I know you're here somewhere, I can hear your teeth chattering.

(BWANA *crashes into a sign. He steps back, trying to read the sign through the binoculars. He steps back further. And further.)*

BWANA *(reading):* The . . . King . . . Dome. We're in *Seattle?* Wait . . . *(Reads again)* . . . The Kingdom! The Kingdom. I found it! Lump! Here boy! I found the Kingdom! (LUMP *hesitantly comes out from hiding.)* We have come to the end of our journey!

(LUMP *comes at him to hug him.* BWANA *is looking the other direction through the binoculars. He turns and sees* LUMP *loom large in the lenses.)*

BWANA: No, Lump! NO!

(LUMP *throws his arms around* BWANA, *ecstatically.* BWANA *gags and pulls free.)*

BWANA: You touched me . . . YOU TOUCHED ME! You know I always get warts when you touch me.

LUMP *(cowering):* I'm sorry . . . Bono.

BWANA: BWANA! My name is Bwana, you imbecile!

(LUMP *whimpers.)*

BWANA: Again.

(LUMP *whimpers louder.*)

BWANA: Better. This is it, Lump. What we've been looking for. The Kingdom!
Just look at it, Lump!

(LUMP *goes to the tunnel and points at it.*)

BWANA: Isn't this just like you. Here we are at the greatest moment of our lives
and you wander off.

(LUMP *points wildly at the tunnel.*)

BWANA: We've traveled so far. We followed the road unerringly. We forsook all
earthly pleasures that were . . . oh so EARTHLY . . . and PLEASURABLE.
Do you remember the pain, Lump?

(LUMP *beats his breast, falls on his knees, acting out the travelog. He crawls toward*
BWANA.)

BWANA: We straggled bone-weary over all those miles. Over hills and plains.
Remember how we hacked through the tangled underbrush that reached
out and pinched our little toes?

(LUMP *pinches* BWANA*'s toes.* BWANA *looks down.*)

BWANA: Stop that! (*Back to the story*) Through the dark forests! Through the
scorching deserts . . .

(LUMP *gets out a kazoo and plays "It's a Long Way to Tipperary" as he marches in cir-
cles.*)

BWANA: . . . through muck and mire. Through field and fountain, moor and
mountain, through the bog, the fog, the smog . . . (*Sees* LUMP *playing and
marching*) Lump?

(LUMP *freezes, kazoo in mouth.*)

BWANA: You were trying to be funny, weren't you? You were using humor.

LUMP (*shy*): Yes . . .

BWANA: How special. How . . . human of you. You know, humor is the thing
that keeps you from being just an animal. Bark, Lump. BARK!

LUMP: Woof.

BWANA: Good boy! And now, it is time we went into the Kingdom. I know new
territory scares you, Lumpy, so I'll go in first. Isn't that thoughtful of me?

LUMP: Yes, Llama.

BWANA: BWANA, you—oh, how can I get angry at a time like this? It's so
worldly. No, we must put that kind of thing . . . behind us . . .

(LUMP *has his head in the tunnel, his rear sticking out.* BWANA *gets a mischievous grin, creeps over, about to boot* LUMP *in the behind—when he sees the sign pointing to the tunnel.)*

BWANA: Oh, no. It can't be. *(Pulls* LUMP *out of the tunnel)* Get outta there! *(He peers inside.)* But this can't be the way in. The signs are wrong. This is so . . . so . . . inauspicious. Where's all the gold and the pearly . . . whatever? And look at this entrance. They haven't given us much room, Lump. Well, here goes. I'll see you on the other side. Farewell, Lump!

*(*BWANA *plunges into the tunnel, still wearing the duffel and carrying the train case. He gets hopelessly wedged in the small entrance. He wiggles, pushes, twists. But he is seriously stuck.)*

BWANA: Lump? You know how I hate tight places. I'm going insane. I'm going absolutely, positively in-SANE! Help me, Lump! I promise I'll never write slanderous letters to your mother again.

*(*LUMP *looks shocked.)*

BWANA: I promise I won't make rude gestures at you while you're sleeping.

*(*LUMP *is outraged.)*

BWANA: I'll give you many, many chocolates!

*(*LUMP *grabs* BWANA*'s feet and starts to push.)*

BWANA: No, you vicious little armadillo! You're pushing me! Don't push—pull! Think backward, Lump. Think backward.

*(*LUMP *stops, thinks, then begins to tug on* BWANA*'s feet.* BWANA *pops out of the tunnel.)*

BWANA: You enjoyed that, didn't you? Get me up!

*(*LUMP *helps* BWANA *to his feet.)*

BWANA: I don't understand this. How are we supposed to get into the Kingdom with all our stuff? This shows very poor design sense.

*(*BWANA *paces, thinking.* LUMP *follows behind him.)*

BWANA: I've got it! Lump, you go through first and I'll hand all this stuff through *(stops)*—wait a minute . . . if you think I'm letting you in there first, you've got another think coming! OK, I'll go in first and you can hand all this stuff through to *(stops)*—oh, you'd just LOVE that, wouldn't you! Me leaving you out here with all this stuff. *(He thinks.)* The wagon!

LUMP: The wagon!

BWANA: The wagon, Lump!

LUMP: The wagon! The wagon!

Bwana: Lump, get the wagon.

Lump: Oh.

(Lump *pulls the wagon over.*)

Bwana: Now we're talkin'.

(*They try and force the full wagon into the entrance. No go.*)

Bwana: What is this! Somebody's idea of a sick joke?

(Bwana *thinks. Then he pulls off his binoculars and hands them to* Lump.)

Bwana: OK, you'll have to bring these through with you, do you understand?

(Lump *nods and puts them around his already loaded neck.* Bwana *dives into the entrance. His duffel and train case stop him. He pulls out.*)

Bwana: This is just sick and wrong! (*Looks up to heaven*) What more do you want of me? This? (*He pulls off his camera.*) Will this do it for you?

(*He hands the camera to* Lump, *who slings it over his shoulder already loaded with several duffels and a train case.*)

Bwana: Treat it as if it were mine.

(Bwana *makes another dive into the entrance. He pushes. He twists. He wriggles.*)

Bwana: It's too small! They made it too small! But we came all this way. Traveled so far. And for this? WHAT ABOUT ALL MY STUFF?

(Bwana *turns to* Lump.)

Bwana: Lump . . . I'm going to do something I've never, ever done before.

(Lump *pulls back, alarmed.*)

Bwana: Please . . . please don't think I'm crazy. But . . . I want to ask . . . your a-a-a- (Lump *whacks him on the back of the head*) ADVICE.

(Lump *reels back, as if struck.*)

Lump: My . . . advice?

Bwana: Yes, your advice.

Lump: You want MY advice, Guano?

Bwana (*winces at the word, but doesn't rise to it*): Yes, Lump. You heard correctly. Tell me what we should do!

(Lump *looks at the entrance. He pulls out a tape measure. Pulls out a calculator. Works up some figures.*)

Bwana: Lump, what are you doing?

(Lump *comes to a decision. He pulls a duffel bag off his shoulder and drops it.*)

Bwana: Lump, that isn't funny.

(Lump *pulls a duffel off the other shoulder and drops it.*)

Bwana: You pick that up, mister!

(Lump *drops the train case.*)

Bwana: PICK IT UP! PICK THAT UP!

(*But* Lump *has gone wild, tearing off satchels and duffels, overcoats, binoculars, cameras . . .* Bwana *scurries behind picking them all up.*)

Bwana: Stop this! Stop the madness! What are you doing? I can't possibly carry all this stuff!

(Lump *is free of everything, except his own pants, shirt, and shoes.*)

Lump: Bye-bye, Bwana.

(Lump *dives into the entrance.*)

Bwana: No!

(Bwana *drops the stuff and grabs* Lump's *foot. There's a tug-of-war.*)

Bwana: Come back here, you ingrate!

(Lump's *shoe comes off and he sails through into the Kingdom.* Lump *yahoos from the other side.* Bwana *stares at the shoe. Sticks his face in the entrance.*)

Bwana: Lump! Lump, you come back here and get all this stuff! LUUUMP! Traitor!

(Bwana *stands. He looks around at all the stuff everywhere.*)

Bwana: What'll I do? What'll I do?

(*Then he gets an idea. He smiles. He grabs the wagon's handle.*)

Bwana: All right . . . so where's the back door?

Blackout

The Very Least

A Sketch Without Words on Giving

Cast

BUSINESSMAN: *any age/gender*
NEEDMAN: *any age/gender*
GODLY LADY: *any age/gender*
ENTREPRENEUR: *any age/gender*

Scene

A city street

Costumes

Modern

Props

Wall Street Journal
Collection can
Christian magazine
Sharper Image catalog
Old crutch
Rope
Water gun
Sign that says: **PLEASE HELP ME!**

Running Time

5-6 minutes

Notes

A sketch on fulfilling Jesus' command to give to others as if you were giving to Him.

"'Lord, when did we see you hungry and feed you, or thirsty and give you something to drink? When did we see you a stranger and invite you in, or needing clothes and clothe you? When did we see you sick or in prison and go to visit you?'

"The King will reply, 'I tell you the truth, whatever you did for one of the least of these brothers of mine, you did for me.'"

Matthew 25:37-40

The sound of a BUSY STREET.

Lights.

The playing area is empty. The sound of a BUSY STREET FADES and the sound of a DRUM BEATING a cadence is heard.

This rhythm will build throughout the scene.

BUSINESSMAN enters. Face buried in a *Wall Street Journal.* Without looking up, he begins marching in a circle, matching the drum's rhythm. He marches alone for a few moments, then:

NEEDMAN comes in. Dressed in rumpled, baggy clothes. His hair is disheveled. He watches BUSINESSMAN for a moment, trying to muster courage. Then the sound of a STOMACH GROWLING. Loud. It's the NEEDMAN's stomach. He decides what to do. He walks up to the BUSINESSMAN, sadly pulls his pockets inside out, and holds out a cupped hand.

BUSINESSMAN breezes past NEEDMAN without noticing him.

NEEDMAN looks at him in dismay. He waits for BUSINESSMAN to make another round, then repeats the same business.

BUSINESSMAN passes, ignoring him.

NEEDMAN is hurt. At the next pass, he mimes holding a baby, then holds up one cupped hand.

BUSINESSMAN passes.

NEEDMAN throws his hands in the air. Looks around. Trying to decide what to do next.

A GODLY LADY enters. Dressed conservatively stylish. She holds a can that reads "God Cares." Her face is buried in a religious magazine. She falls into step behind BUSINESSMAN, several feet behind him.

NEEDMAN sees the GODLY LADY. Sees the can. Reads it. He's overjoyed! He shakes his pocket lining, holds out a cupped hand.

The GODLY LADY passes him.

NEEDMAN is flabbergasted. He follows her. He points to heaven. He points at his stomach.

GODLY LADY ignores him.

NEEDMAN falls to his knees.

BUSINESSMAN and GODLY LADY pass him by.

NEEDMAN throws his arms out in exasperation. He looks up to heaven, pleading.

An ENTREPRENEUR enters, dressed J. Crew and face buried in a *Sharper Image* catalog. He falls in step a few feet behind GODLY LADY.

NEEDMAN sees ENTREPRENEUR. He claps with joy and runs up to him. He shows his pockets. Offers his cupped hand.

50

Entrepreneur ignores him.

Needman panics. He runs after him, falling to his knees, imploring. Then catches up to him, falling on his knees again. Imploring.

But Needman stays on his knees a little too long. Businessman steps right on him and keeps walking. Needman picks himself up. Dusts himself off. Turns in time to see Godly Lady bearing down on him. He jumps out of her way, right into the path of Entrepreneur.

Now Needman is caught in the middle of the circle. He cuts across the sphere, trying to get someone's attention. Finally, he collapses. Exhausted. Gets a hunger spasm. Grabs his stomach and winces. He's at wit's end.

Suddenly, Needman jumps up and dashes off. He comes in holding up a cardboard sign: **PLEASE HELP ME!**

No one notices.

Needman dashes off. Returns with a battered crutch. He hobbles after them, holding out a hand.

No one notices.

Needman dashes off, returns with a rope. He pretends to string himself up. He hangs there, rope around his throat, eyes closed, tongue hanging out.

No one notices.

Needman dashes off and returns with a gun.

No one notices.

He points it at his temple.

No one notices.

He drops the gun from his head, inadvertently pointing it at them on the way down.

Businessman sees the gun and freezes in terror. He drops his *Wall Street Journal*, steps out of cadence, and throws up his hands.

Needman looks at him, confused.

Businessman turns to the other two, shouting for help.

The other two don't notice him.

Businessman finally begs for his life, yanks out his wallet, fishes out his money, and holds it out in the air for Needman.

Needman stares at him, astonished. He shrugs and reaches for the proferred cash.

The Godly Lady, passing by, sees the money and snatches it. She stuffs the money in her collection can, shakes the Businessman's hand, and keeps going.

Needman and Businessman look at her, mouths dropped open in amazement.

Businessman then turns to Needman and begs for his life. Needman looks confused, then sees he is still holding the gun. Needman laughs, points the gun at Businessman, and shoots him in the face with a stream of water.

Needman laughs, uproariously.

Businessman grabs Needman by the throat, shakes him around, tosses him aside.

Needman picks himself up, dusts himself off. He glares at the Businessman.

Businessman pulls out his pockets making rabbit ears. He looks up to heaven, imploring. Then he turns to NEEDMAN and holds his hand out for some change.

NEEDMAN sadly shakes his head. Points to his own pocket rabbit ears.

BUSINESSMAN looks around, frustrated. He sees GODLY LADY and ENTREPRENEUR still marching in a circle. BUSINESSMAN goes to them, holding out a cupped hand.

GODLY LADY ignores him.

ENTREPRENEUR ignores him.

BUSINESSMAN turns to NEEDMAN with a look of shock. NEEDMAN shrugs, nods his head, wearily.

BUSINESSMAN goes back to the GODLY LADY and the ENTREPRENEUR. Holds out his hand. He's soundly ignored. BUSINESSMAN picks up the pace, falls in step alongside the ENTREPRENEUR, holding out his hand.

ENTREPRENEUR picks up his pace.

NEEDMAN watches this. Gets a hunger pang and grabs his stomach.

BUSINESSMAN falls in step with the GODLY LADY. Holds out his hand. She picks up her pace. BUSINESSMAN picks up his pace to match her.

NEEDMAN sits down. He's too hungry to move.

BUSINESSMAN moves from GODLY LADY to the ENTREPRENEUR. The circle gets faster and faster and faster.

NEEDMAN watches the sight. Holding his stomach. Finally, he closes his eyes.

The circle goes faster and faster.

And the lights fade to

Blackout

Mine Games

A Sketch Without Words on Greed

Cast

ONE: *any age/gender*
TWO: *any age/gender*

Scene

Anywhere

Costumes

Modern

Props

Black blocks or crates
A banner on a pole—a fabric streamer 6' long

Running Time

5 minutes

Notes

This is an adaptation of an ancient South American theatre piece on the dangers of greed. It comes out of an improvisation acting game where the only word used to convey emotion is "Hey."

> "But the worries of this life, the deceitfulness of wealth and the desires for other things come in and choke the word, making it unfruitful."
> **Mark 4:19**

The playing area is littered with black boxes or crates. On top of one of the boxes is a pole with a long, thin banner hanging from it.

One enters from somewhere. Looks around. Scratches his head. Looks around some more. Then he cups his hand and shouts, "Hey!"

His "Hey" echoes. But no one returns the call. One shouts "Hey!" again. Echoes. No return call. One shrugs, sadly. Starts to walk off.

"Hey!" is shouted back to him from somewhere.

One is shocked. But he's suspicious. He cautiously calls out, "Hey!"

"Hey!" is returned. One grins. He runs around shouting "Hey!" A "Hey!" is always returned from somewhere. This "Heying" goes on for a moment. One doesn't seem to notice that the other "Hey!" is getting louder. Faster. Closer.

One reaches the blocks. He shouts "Hey!"

No reply.

One shouts "Hey!" again.

No reply.

One looks sad. He lost his friend. He's alone. He starts to walk away, dejectedly.

Suddenly Two springs up from behind a block, shouting "HEY!"

One shouts "HEY!" in terror and jumps behind a block. Two drops down behind his block too.

One pops up his head, snaps out a threatening "Hey!"

Two pops his head up and returns the "Hey!" defensively.

They both drop down behind their blocks. They repeat their territorial "Hey!" a couple of times. Finally, they creep out and advance on one another. Their "Heys" are like low growls. Tomcats protecting their turf. They circle each other.

Then One cautiously reaches out and touches Two's nose. Then he touches his own nose. He grins and says "Hey!" in surprised joy.

Two does the same, touching One's nose.

One reaches out and touches Two's hand. Finally, they shake, both saying "Hey!" in delighted tones.

Then they stop and look at each other. They smile. They laugh. They point at each other and say "Hey," as in "you ol' rascal."

Two reaches out a finger and pokes One in the eye. One recoils: "Hey!" Holds his eye in pain.

Two looks at his finger and laughs.

One sticks out his finger to eye-poke Two in reciprocation.

Two doubles up his fist at him and says, "Hey!" as in "Just TRY it."

One retreats, points at his eye and whines, "Heeey!"

Two laughs. One finally angrily bellows "HEY!" Two bellows "HEY!" back. They angrily bark "HEY!" at each other, getting louder and more warlike.

They start to walk away from each other. They snap around and say, "HEY!" like a father playing peek-a-boo.

They both laugh and fall on the ground. Repeat this business a couple of times until . . .

Both of them see the banner on the pole stuck in the block.

They both say "Hey!" simultaneously. They both scramble to the banner, kicking and pushing each other aside to get to it.

Two gets there first and grabs the banner. He cries out "Hey!" in victory and jumps to the ground. He leaps around, holding the banner just out of ONE's reach and chanting, "Hey! Hey! Hey!"

ONE follows TWO around, petulantly. He wants the banner. He tries to grab it. He can't get it. TWO keeps dancing around, taunting him with "Heys!"

ONE gets an idea. He stands on a block and when TWO passes by, he snatches the banner out of his hand. ONE jumps off the block, dancing and laughing with the banner in his hand.

TWO says, "Hey!"

ONE keeps dancing. TWO climbs up on a block and snags the banner out of ONE's hand. ONE continues dancing, not realizing he doesn't have the banner anymore. ONE then stops, looks at his empty hand: "Hey . . ."

TWO shouts a triumphal "HEY!" from atop the block.

ONE looks up at him in anger: "Hey!"

TWO looks down. Sees the menace in ONE's eyes. He jumps off the block and starts running, both shouting "Hey!" "Hey!" "Hey!" "Hey!"

TWO stays one step ahead of ONE. Finally, TWO is cornered. ONE advances on him, menacingly. TWO thrusts and parries the pole-and-banner as if it were a sword.

ONE catches hold of the banner and pulls it toward him.

TWO shouts: "Hey!" And pulls it back.

They repeat this business several times. It becomes more and more savage.

Finally, ONE rips the banner out of TWO's hands. TWO screams "Hey!" and grabs his injured hand.

ONE dances around shouting, "Hey, hey, hey!" in triumph. TWO whimpers "Hey . . . hey . . . hey" at the pain and injustice.

Then ONE accidentally drops the banner. It falls between them.

They both stare at it.

They scramble for it. TWO gets to it first, jumps to his feet, holding the banner high and shouting "HEY!" in utter triumph.

ONE comes up behind TWO, clasps his hands together, and with an angry "HEY!" brings his fist down hard on TWO's shoulder.

TWO screams "HEEEY!" and drops the banner. He falls to his knees, clutching his shoulder.

ONE grabs the banner and dances around, taunting TWO with "Hey, Hey, Hey!"

TWO feebly reaches up for the banner with his good hand.

ONE smacks the pole-and-banner down on TWO's head with an angry "Hey!"

TWO pitches forward, unconscious.

ONE is manic with victory, wildly leaping around and shouting: "Hey! Hey! Hey!" He whips the banner around like a lasso. It begins to wrap around his body. He doesn't notice. He continues shouting "Hey, Hey, Hey!"

But the banner has wound all the way around him. He cries out "Hey?" in sudden realization. But it's too late.

The banner wraps around his neck. It cinches tight. His last "He—?" is cut short.

Freeze.

Blackout

In Charge

A Sketch Without Words on Faithfulness

Cast

Servant
Master

Scene

The Master's House

Props

Colored blocks, crates, or chairs
Broom
Carpetbag
Big old-fashioned key
Party favors
Party hat
Confetti
Wooden shelf with sign **LIQUOR CABINET**
Bottles
Wicker basket
Clothes

Running Time

6-7 minutes

Notes

This is a comically disturbing sketch based on a difficult scripture about the cost of faithlessness.

Production Notes

This scene is done in broad pantomime style. Costumes can be clowny and baggy, or basic black with a bright coat and hat. They should be attention-getting. You will need to make sound effects for the piece with piano, slide whistles, bongos, cymbals, recorders, etc.

"Who then is the faithful and wise servant, whom the master has put in charge of the servants in his household to give them their food at the proper time? It will be good for that servant whose master finds him doing so when he returns. I tell you the truth, he will put him in charge of all his possessions. But suppose that servant is wicked and says to himself, 'My master is staying away a long time,' and he then begins to beat his fellow servants and to eat and drink with drunkards. The master of that servant will come on a day when he does not expect him and at an hour he is not aware of. He will cut him to pieces and assign him a place with the hypocrites, where there will be weeping and gnashing of teeth."

Matthew 24:45-51

Lights.

Groups of colored blocks, crates, or chairs set around creating pieces of furniture in a house. There's also a wicker basket. And a wooden shelf marked **LIQUOR CABINET.**

SERVANT enters carrying a broom. Looks around the room. Sighs in contentment. Makes a cursory attempt at sweeping, then brushes off his rear with the broom and sits.

He smiles. He gets an idea.

He plays as if he were an imperious king. He uses the broom as a scepter. He dispenses blessings with it. Touches the head of each kneeling subject, knighting them. He laughs with glee.

MASTER enters, calling the SERVANT.

SERVANT jumps up, the broom flies out of his hand. It lands on the ground. MASTER and SERVANT look at it.

MASTER sighs and picks up the broom. Carries it to SERVANT and holds it out to him. SERVANT falls to the floor and cringes, expects a beating. He peeks with one eye. Sees the broom held out to him, smiles and takes it. SERVANT hugs the MASTER's legs in relief.

MASTER pries SERVANT off him. The SERVANT stands. The MASTER motions for him to "Wait here." MASTER turns to go.

SERVANT follows.

MASTER stops him and again motions for him to "Wait here." MASTER turns to go. SERVANT follows.

MASTER whirls around, SERVANT freezes.

MASTER goes out.

(*A beat*)

He returns with a large carpetbag. He sets it down, motions for SERVANT to come to him.

SERVANT goes to MASTER with a puzzled look. MASTER mimes that he's going on a long journey. Far away. Many days.

SERVANT looks terrifically sad. Then he asides to us a quick moment of glee about having his run of the place.

MASTER starts to walk away, motions for SERVANT to follow him. SERVANT follows, close on his heels. MASTER stops. SERVANT plows into him. MASTER patiently, as a hundred times before, relocates SERVANT to a more negotiable distance.

MASTER picks up a broom and mimes sweeping the floor. He points to SERVANT.

SERVANT nods his head.

MASTER looks incredulous, but hands SERVANT the broom. MASTER walks away. SERVANT looks at the broom, then tosses it.

MASTER opens the wicker basket and pulls out clothes. He mimes for SERVANT to wash them.

SERVANT vigorously nods his head.

MASTER turns his head away. SERVANT laughs and asides to us his best "as if" look.

MASTER goes to the bed and mimes making it up. He points at SERVANT.

SERVANT nods his head with relish.

MASTER walks away. SERVANT lies on the bed. MASTER goes to the shelf marked **LIQUOR CABINET.** He sees SERVANT asleep on the bed. He calls SERVANT's name. SERVANT leaps out of bed, looking around for the monster. He sees MASTER glaring at him, shrugs and grins.

MASTER points at the "Liquor Cabinet" and shakes his head "no."

SERVANT smiles and shakes his head "YES!" The MASTER shakes his head "NO!" Then he mimes closing the cabinet doors and locking them with a Big Key. He puts the Big Key in his back pocket and turns to walk away.

SERVANT grabs the Big Key out of MASTER's back pocket and hides it under his shirt. SERVANT follows MASTER. Too close. MASTER stops and bends over to pick up his carpetbag. SERVANT plows into him, knocking him down. The mortified SERVANT helps MASTER up, starts dusting him off with the broom.

MASTER stops SERVANT and picks up his carpetbag. He waves good-bye to SERVANT.

SERVANT weeps and hugs his MASTER. He slides down to his knees and clutches his MASTER's legs. MASTER disengages himself and leaves.

SERVANT runs to the door, watching him go.

MASTER turns back, giving SERVANT one last motion of admonishment and goes.

SERVANT waves sadly. When MASTER is out of sight, SERVANT slams the door and does a dance. A big liberation number.

MASTER comes back in, heading for the door.

SERVANT whips out the Big Key and heads for the "Liquor Cabinet," dancing all the way. He almost has the Big Key fitted in the door.

MASTER comes in.

SERVANT quickly turns his dance into wails. He collapses in tears on the floor. MASTER comes over, taps him on the shoulder. SERVANT sees the MAS-

TER, jumps up, and hugs him. MASTER pulls SERVANT off and holds out his hand.

SERVANT drops his head, pulls out the Big Key, and drops it in MASTER's hand.

MASTER leaves, slamming the door.

SERVANT stands there, dejected.

SERVANT grabs the broom and starts sweeping. He sweeps. He sweeps some more. Now he's worked up a thirst. He sweeps past the "Liquor Cabinet." He looks at it. Shakes his head "no," and keeps sweeping. He looks at the "Liquor Cabinet" again. He's so thirsty. He looks around. He sweeps the broom so the handle of the broom breaks the "Liquor Cabinet" glass.

Sound of GLASS SHATTERING.

SERVANT feigns shock. He goes to the "Liquor Cabinet," looks around, then yanks a bottle out. He knocks back a long slug. He ducks, waiting for the retribution sure to come. Nothing. He opens an eye and looks to heaven. Nothing. No one's watching.

He slugs back another drink. Winces again. Looks to heaven. No one.

He laughs. He takes another long drink. He kisses the broom and flings it. He pulls a party favor out of his back pocket and blows it. He pulls a handful of confetti out of his pocket and slings it into the air. He dances around.

Sound of DOORBELL RINGING.

The SERVANT pulls a party hat out of his back pocket and puts it on. He throws open the door.

Sound of PARTY CACOPHONY.

SERVANT shakes hands with each "person" coming into the room, making it obvious when a "woman" comes in. He toots his party favor. Drinks. Makes jokes. Throws confetti. He reaches into the "Liquor Cabinet" and hands out bottles to everyone. More toots on the party favor. More confetti.

SERVANT becomes tired. Exhausted. He falls on the bed in a drunken sleep.

Sound of DOORBELL RINGING.

SERVANT jumps out of bed. He's not quite as jaunty as the day before. Hung over. He drinks. Hands out bottles. Dances a jig. Knocks furniture over. Toots the party favor. Throws confetti.

Then SERVANT collapses on the bed again.

Sound of DOORBELL RINGING.

SERVANT jumps up. Does it all again—but wearily. Dancing. Drinking. Now SERVANT barely has enough breath to blow out the party favor. Can barely toss confetti.

MASTER appears, walking toward the door. Back from his trip.

SERVANT is on his last legs.

MASTER hears the party noise and quickens his step. He throws open the door. The noise abruptly stops. MASTER is spun around as "people" race out of the room.

SERVANT is standing there. Weaving. The party favor unfurled, looking like a tongue. Wondering where everyone's going.

Then SERVANT sees MASTER.

SERVANT drops the favor. He scrambles around, looking for the broom. He finds it, starts sweeping up the place. He tries to put bottles back into the "Liquor Cabinet."

SERVANT looks at MASTER.

MASTER shakes his head.

SERVANT panics. He puts some furniture right. He looks at MASTER.

MASTER points for SERVANT to leave.

SERVANT doesn't budge.

MASTER walks to him and takes hold of his broom. SERVANT won't let go. There's a struggle. MASTER wins. He pulls the broom away from SERVANT.

MASTER grimly points to the door.

SERVANT grabs MASTER. Weeps. Slides down to his knees, hugging the MASTER's knees.

MASTER pulls out of SERVANT's grip and stands him on his feet. He walks SERVANT to the door. MASTER opens the door.

SERVANT dejectedly walks outside. Then SERVANT spins around and tries to run back in.

MASTER slams the door shut.

SERVANT pounds on it.

MASTER sadly begins to sweep the place up, righting furniture.

SERVANT pounds on the door.

MASTER continues to sweep, grimly ignoring SERVANT.

SERVANT stops knocking. He takes off his party hat and lays it on the doorstep.

SERVANT goes to knock again. Stops himself.

SERVANT sits down on the stoop. He drops his head in his hands.

MASTER continues grimly sweeping up the room as the lights begin to . . .

But just before darkness—the MASTER stops sweeping and looks out at SERVANT. He has a look of compassion on his face.

And then

Blackout

61

0 Shopping Days

A Sketch Without Words for Christmas

Cast

CLERK: *a man of any age*
SHOPPER ONE: *a woman of any age*
SHOPPER TWO: *a woman of any age*

Scene

A department store

Props

Sale table
A sign: **0 SHOPPING DAYS**
Sweater
Store bags
Purses
Wallets
Cash
Photos
Christmas lists

Costumes

Modern

Running Time

5 minutes

Notes

A sketch that says family is more important than stuff at Christmas.

Production Notes

This sketch can be used in a mall or as a lead-in to a Christmas sermon. The arms of the sweater need to be "scored" (partially cut) in order for them to tear off at the right moment.

Jaunty holiday music, perhaps from *The Nutcracker.*
Lights.
A department store table on Christmas Eve. This late in the evening, there is only a sweater left. Above the table a sign that reads: **0 SHOPPING DAYS.**
A CLERK comes in, checks the table, checks his watch, and walks off.
SHOPPER ONE and SHOPPER TWO rush in from opposite sides of the playing area. They have huge lists in hand. Several department store shopping bags hang on their arms.
The CLERK passes SHOPPER ONE, points to his watch, and motions, "Five minutes till closing." SHOPPER ONE panics.
The CLERK passes SHOPPER TWO and does the same thing: "Five minutes till closing." SHOPPER TWO goes into a terror.
SHOPPER ONE spots the table.
SHOPPER TWO spots the table.
They don't spot each other. Both SHOPPERS rush to the table.
SHOPPER ONE grabs one arm of the sweater and starts to run off. SHOPPER TWO grabs the other arm of the sweater and runs off in the other direction. They yank to a dead stop, like a tug-of-war, and turn to see each other.
SHOPPER ONE motions that the sweater is hers. SHOPPER TWO motions the sweater is *hers.*
SHOPPER ONE tugs the sweater her way. SHOPPER TWO tugs the sweater back. Back, forth. Back, forth. Back, forth.
They glare at each other. They snarl. They spin in a circle, tugging and pulling. Then they circle face-to-face. Nose to nose. Will it come to blows?
The CLERK enters and walks by.
SHOPPER ONE and SHOPPER TWO quickly make it look as if they are holding the sweater up against each other, checking the size. They smile and chatter like old friends.
The CLERK eyes them a moment, then goes out.
SHOPPER ONE and SHOPPER TWO immediately separate and begin circling one another, gripping each arm of the sweater.
Then they stop. They look at each other. They smile. SHOPPER ONE motions that SHOPPER TWO can have the sweater. No, no, SHOPPER TWO motions back: you take the sweater. They both laugh and pretend to loosen their grip on it.
Then the SHOPPERS suddenly race off in opposite directions, hoping to get the sweater.
The arms of the sweater rip off. The body of the sweater falls on the floor between them.
The SHOPPERS both look off. They see the CLERK coming. They grab the sweater off the floor and quickly make it look like both arms are on the sweater.
The CLERK enters and walks by.

The SHOPPERS smile and admire the sweater, which doesn't look the least bit damaged.

The CLERK goes out.

The SHOPPERS motion how the other ruined the sweater. They glare at each other. They motion that the other should pay for it. Then they make a big deal of dropping the ruined garment back on the sale table and turning their noses up it—and at each other.

They turn in a huff and walk off.

They reach the sides of the stage. They look back to see if the other is looking. They see each other. Glare. Then walk out of the store.

Quiet. Nothing.

Both SHOPPERS bolt in for the sweater.

SHOPPER ONE gets the body of the sweater and an arm. SHOPPER TWO just gets an arm. SHOPPER ONE thinks she has the whole sweater and laughs at SHOPPER TWO—who grins and holds up the missing arm. SHOPPER ONE is sad. Then mad. Then sad.

SHOPPER ONE holds up her list, showing SHOPPER TWO how long it is. SHOPPER TWO holds up her list, displaying how many names are on it.

SHOPPER TWO motions that they should make a trade. SHOPPER ONE agrees. SHOPPER TWO hands SHOPPER ONE the missing arm, and SHOPPER ONE hands SHOPPER TWO the sweater body.

They start to go. Then see that one of them has two sweater arms and the other the body.

SHOPPER TWO hands SHOPPER ONE the body of the sweater, and takes the two arms. They start to go. But they stop and see it's separated arms and body again.

Then they face off, windmilling pieces back and forth, hoping one of them will somehow snag all the pieces at one time and run.

The CLERK comes in. He sees the SHOPPERS and is astounded. He stops to watch.

The SHOPPERS don't see him. They keep up with their piece-trading back and forth: One arm, one body; two arms, no body, etc.

The CLERK whistles.

The SHOPPERS freeze. One is holding the sweater arms. One is holding the body. They look at the CLERK. Immediately the SHOPPERS point at each other, blaming the other for ripping the sweater. They motion how the other destroyed the sweater.

The CLERK whistles.

The SHOPPERS stop.

The CLERK holds out his hands. He wants the sweater pieces.

The SHOPPERS look at each other, suspicious about who will give up their pieces first. They start to hold out their sweater piece, then pull back. Hold out, then pull back.

The CLERK snatches the pieces away from them.

The SHOPPERS glare at the CLERK.

The CLERK motions that SHOPPER ONE must pay for the sweater arms. And SHOPPER TWO must pay for the sweater body.

The Shoppers look indignant, pointing at each other in blame for the sweater's ruination.

The Clerk holds up a big whistle about to blow it to call security.

The Shoppers stop bickering.

The Clerk motions for the money again.

The Shoppers slowly the reach into their purses. They pull out wallets, throwing eye-darts at each other. They pull out cash and glare at each other as they hand the money to the Clerk.

The Clerk tugs. Neither Shopper will let go of the money. Finally, the Clerk yanks the bills out of their hands.

The Shoppers start to close up their wallets. Shopper One looks over at Shopper Two's wallet, notices something. She points inside Shopper Two's wallet. Shopper Two looks in her wallet and nods. Then she smiles.

Shopper Two pulls out of her wallet what Shopper One pointed at: A photo of her grandchildren.

The Shoppers admire the photo. Shopper Two motions the ages of her grandchildren.

Shopper One pulls a photo out of her wallet. Shopper Two takes it, looks it over, and smiles. Shopper One motions the ages of *her* grandchildren.

The Clerk watches this, astounded.

The Shoppers trade photos back and forth. They laugh. They smile. They coo. They sit on the empty Sale Table, looking at each other's photos.

The Clerk looks at them. Shrugs. Puts the money in his pocket. Looks at the sweater. Holds it up to himself. Checks the arms. He smiles. He puts the sweater in a department store bag. Then he pulls a Christmas list out of his back pocket, checks off a name. Grins. Walks out.

The Shoppers are left, smiling at the pictures, laughing, talking about their families like the best of friends.

As the lights fade to

Blackout

Free Your Mime

An Evangelism Sketch for Easter

Cast

MIME: *any age/gender*
PANTO: *any age/gender*
FREEMIME: *any age/gender*

Scene

Anywhere

Costumes

Old-school mime (black)

Props

A rag
Makeup

Running Time

6-7 minutes

Notes

This sketch has fun with old-school mime bits in order to tell the story of
Christ's salvation.

Production Notes

You do *not* have to be fluent in mime or clowning to pull this sketch off.

(MIME *comes in dressed in old-school black and whiteface. He performs that old mime
chestnut "The Box." Traces the flat of his hand along the dimensions of "The Box" he's*

trapped in. He gets more disturbed as he finds no exit. Do this until an audience gathers.

(PANTO *enters from an upper level of the mall or from across the street. He's in an old-school mime costume as well, but he's wiping the clown white off his face with a rag. He shouts at the* MIME.)

PANTO: Hey, what're you doin' down there? Knock it off!

(MIME *stops what he's doing and looks up.* PANTO *runs down to where* MIME *is.*)

PANTO: Oh, gimme a break. You're not doin' that old-school mime stuff, are ya? Get off it. That bit's older than Marcel Marceau. And even *he* doesn't do it anymore.

(MIME *shows* PANTO *how he's trapped, flatting his hand against the walls of the invisible box.*)

PANTO: Yeah, yeah, you're trapped in (*Making quotes*) "The Box." Look, let's get a couple of things straight, OK? First of all, people don't like mimes. They're spooky. They scare children and old people. And second, people really hate mimes who do "The Old Box Routine."

(MIME *shakes his head and frantically continues to flat his hand against his invisible prison.*)

PANTO: You're really not gonna say nothin', are ya? You're really gonna play this bit to the hilt, aren't ya? (*He turns to the audience.*) What're ya gonna do, huh? Mimes are not like normal people, y'know? All that Kabuki makeup does somethin' to the brain.

(*To* MIME)

You're *not* trapped in there, OK? I just stepped out of a box over there. Ya don't need to do this. Trust me. Just step out and Free Your Mime.

(MIME *straightens and looks at him, incredulous.*)

PANTO: That's right. Just walk out. One foot in front of the other. Like a normal person.

(MIME *smiles. He walks toward* PANTO. *He hits the invisible wall and falls on his backside.* MIME *starts to cry.*)

PANTO: Aw, don't do that! If there's one thing people hate to see, it's a crying mime. It's pathetic. Knock it off!

(MIME *stops crying.*)

PANTO: Ya want me to show you you're not trapped, huh?

(MIME *nods his head.*)

PANTO: Come on, just say "Yes." C'mon, saaaayit.

(MIME *nods his head "Yes."*)

PANTO: I thought you'd do that. OK, watch.

(PANTO *goes to the outside of "The Box" and sticks his hand right through.* MIME *goes wide-eyed.*)

PANTO: See that? Magic, huh? Now watch. I'm gonna step right into your Condo of the Mime and I'm gonna walk you out of there, got it? OK, here I come.

(PANTO *steps inside, then holds his hands up like "Voilà!"* MIME *jumps to his feet. He laughs, dances. Then he grabs* PANTO's *hand and makes a big deal of pumping his arm in joy.* PANTO *pulls his hand free.*)

PANTO: OK, we got it. You're happy. Don't oversell it. All right, let's go, pasty face.

(PANTO *trudges forward. He hits "The Wall."* MIME *plows into him from behind, falling on his backside.*)

PANTO: Aw, man! Not again! Every time I think I'm out of one box I get stuck in another!

(*He turns on* MIME.)

PANTO: YOU!

(MIME *scurries away, terrified.*)

PANTO: You lured me in here 'cuz you didn't wanna be in here alone, huh?

(MIME *shakes his head "No."*)

PANTO: I hate mimes! OK, Mr. Zinc Oxide, how about helpin' me find a way outta here. Well, don't just sit there! Start doin' "The Old Box" routine!

(MIME *jumps up. He and* PANTO *start flatting their hands around the dimensions of the box. Nothing doing. No way out. Then* FREEMIME *comes into the playing area through the audience. He's wearing the usual mime getup, but he's got on a pair of red suspenders.* MIME *sees* FREEMIME *first. They look at each other. They "mirror" hands for a moment, then* MIME *turns and starts to call* PANTO. PANTO, *of course, can't hear him.* MIME *waves, he mimes whistling, he jumps up and down.* PANTO *doesn't see him. Finally,* MIME *tugs on* PANTO's *arm.* PANTO *turns and sees* MIME *pointing off, excitedly.*)

PANTO: What is it, Lassie? You found somethin', boy?

(MIME *points at* FREEMIME. PANTO *sees him.*)

PANTO: Hey, what is this? Mime Central? Get outta here! This is our space. Just move you and your box somewhere else, got it?

(FREEMIME *moves around freely, showing he's not confined.*)

PANTO: Hey, you're out of the box, jack? What's up with that? You know somethin' we don't?

(FREEMIME *nods.*)

PANTO: OK, so give us a hand.

(FREEMIME *holds one hand out to his side.*)

PANTO: OK, give us another hand.

(FREEMIME *holds both hands out to the side. Now he's made a cross with his arms.*)

PANTO: That it? That's all you're gonna do?

(FREEMIME *shakes his head. He walks to "The Box" wall. He looks around the walls for just the right spot.*)

PANTO: So? Can ya break us out?

(FREEMIME *holds up a finger, saying "Watch me." Then he traces a big circle on the face of the wall. Then he grabs the circumference of the circle and rolls it away.* FREEMIME *sticks his hand through the newly created hole into the box.*)

PANTO: Whoa! Did you see that? He opened up a hole! That's impossible!

(FREEMIME *beckons* PANTO *to come out.*)

PANTO: I can just walk out?

(FREEMIME *nods.*)

PANTO: You're not playin' Mime Games with me, are ya?

(FREEMIME *shakes his head.* PANTO *goes to the hole. He sticks his hand through. He grins. Then he sticks both hands through. He laughs. Then he crouches down and steps his entire body through the hole. He stands up on the outside.* PANTO *laughs and shakes* FREEMIME's *hand.*)

PANTO: You did it! You got us out! No more four walls! How'd you do that?

(PANTO *pulls his hand away from* FREEMIME's *grip.* PANTO *looks at* FREEMIME's *hand.* PANTO's *face goes serious. He looks at* FREEMIME. *They look at each other.* PANTO *holds up* FREEMIME's *hand. Now there's a red "wound" visible.*)

PANTO: I see.

(PANTO *turns to* MIME.)

PANTO: OK, Paleface, let's get outta Dodge.

(MIME *huddles up against one wall, crouches down, and shakes his head.*)

PANTO: Oh, come on! There's a hole right there, can't ya see it? It's right there—
oh, I get it. You're one'a those guys that likes to *look* for a way out, but
never wants to *find* a way out. Too bad.

(PANTO *turns to* FREEMIME.)

PANTO: You can't make 'im come out, can ya?

(FREEMIME *shakes his head.*)

PANTO: I guess not. Well, let's get outta here. You lead the way.

(FREEMIME *nods and walks off.* PANTO *starts to follow him, then turns and walks back to "The Box." He crawls into it through the hole.* MIME *looks stunned at the feat.*)

PANTO: Just don't stay in here too long, huh? The walls got a way of closin' in on ya.

(PANTO *draws a coffin-shaped box around* MIME. MIME *looks terrified.* PANTO *turns to go. He walks to "The Wall" and crashes into it. He falls back. He looks back at* MIME, *wide-eyed. Then* PANTO *smiles. He remembers. He finds the hole again and crawls out.* PANTO *stands, dusts himself off.*)

PANTO (*yelling off*): Hey, wait up!

(PANTO *rushes off after* FREEMIME. MIME *looks around, nervously. He goes to the hole and peers out. He shakes his head and steps back.* MIME *starts to flat his hand against the walls looking for a way out. Just like the beginning of the scene.*)

Blackout